WORDS
OF LIFE
& LOVE

2004-2005 NMI
MISSION EDUCATION RESOURCES

❊ ❊ ❊

READING BOOKS

A DANGEROUS DEVOTION
Ordinary People in Extraordinary Adventures
by Carol Anne Eby

AFRICAN MOONS
by Juanita Moon

BEHIND THE VEIL
Taking Christ to Pakistanis
by Dallas Mucci

THE ROOKIE
Reflections of a New Missionary
by Tim Crutcher

TAKIN' IT TO THE STREETS
by Joe Colaizzi

WORDS OF LIFE AND LOVE
World Mission Literature Ministries
by Keith Schwanz

❊ ❊ ❊

ADULT MISSION EDUCATION RESOURCE BOOK

THE MISSION CALL
Edited by Wes Eby

WORDS OF LIFE & LOVE

WORLD MISSION LITERATURE MINISTRIES

KEITH SCHWANZ

NPH

Nazarene Publishing House
Kansas City, Missouri

Copyright 2004
by Nazarene Publishing House

ISBN 083-412-0828

Printed in the United States of America

Editor: Wes Eby
Cover Design: Paul Franitza

10 9 8 7 6 5 4 3 2 1

DEDICATION

I dedicate this book to my father,
the Rev. Leroy C. Schwanz,
who has read every available
missionary reading book for decades.
In his retirement he eagerly circulates the books
among the others in the facility
for prime-timers where he resides.

CONTENTS

As a child, Keith Schwanz first attended a General Assembly of the Church of the Nazarene at the 1964 gathering in Portland, Oregon. His father was a pastor on the Oregon Pacific District at the time, and the family drove to the services several days. Keith remembers wandering through the exhibition area and collecting pamphlets and mementos from the mission displays.

In recent years the adventure of cross-cultural ministry is seen in Keith's leadership of Work and Witness teams, consulting with World Mission Literature Ministries and JESUS Film Harvest Partners, and directing the English as a second language (ESL) ministry at College Church of the Nazarene in Olathe, Kansas.

Dr. Schwanz is an ordained elder in the Church of the Nazarene and has served as a pastor on the Oregon Pacific and Washington Pacific Districts. He is the author of *The Birth of a Hymn: Spiritual Biographies of 20 Hymn Writers and the Experiences That Inspired Them,* a companion to the *Sing to the Lord* hymnal. As a freelance writer, he has penned numerous articles for *Holiness Today, Herald of Holiness, Illustrated Bible Life,* and *The Preacher's Magazine.*

Keith is married to Dr. Judi Schwanz, professor of pastoral care and counseling at Nazarene Theological Seminary. They live in Overland Park, Kansas, and are the parents of two adult children, Karla and Jason.

ACKNOWLEDGMENTS

Many people assisted me as I gathered information to use in writing this book:

- Ray Hendrix, director of World Mission Literature Ministries, suggested key people to contact and responded to countless E-mail messages.
- The World Mission Literature Ministries staff provided access to resources: Karen Phillips, Deanna Bailey, and Pat Braselton.
- Missionaries, both active and retired, gave me a glimpse of life on the field: Carla and Chuck Sunberg, Edna Lochner, Fae Hendrix, John Haines, Neville Bartle, and Nikolaj Sawatzky.
- Educators talked about their experiences in a cross-cultural setting: Al Truesdale, John Nielson, Mario Zani, and Wesley Tracy.
- NIVSers and other persons committed to missions provided insight: Barb Najarian, Gene and Ronoyce Grate, Matthew Robertson, and Maurine Dickerson.

I express my gratitude to my wife, Judi, for being the first editor to sharpen the manuscript.

PRONUNCIATION GUIDE

The following information is provided to assist in pronouncing unfamiliar words in this book. The suggested pronunciations, though not always precise, are close approximations of the way the terms are pronounced.

Büsingen	BOO-zin-guhn
Casa Nazarena de Publicaciones	CAH-sah nahs-ah-RAY-nah day poo-blee-KAH-see-OH-nays
Castillo, Moises	kahs-TEE-yoh, MOI-says
Cobán	koh-BAHN
El Heraldo de Santidad	el ay-RAHL-doh day sahn-tee-DAHD
Gusztin, Imre Mária	GOO-stuhn, EHM-ree MAH-ree-uh
K'ekchí	kek-CHEE
La Hora Nazarena	lah OH-rah nahz-ah-RAY-nah
Luzon	loo-ZOHN
logos of theos	LOH-gahs uhv THEE-ahs
Marduk	MAHR-duhk
Psaute	puh-SOO-tee
Reza, Honorato	RAY-sah, oh-noh-RAH-toh
Sawatsky, Nikolaj	suh-VAHT-skee, NIK-oh-lie
Shangaan	shahn-GAHN
Visayan	vuh-SIE-yuhn
Wiesen	WIE-zuhn
Waray-Waray	WAHR-ie WAHR-ie
Zagreb	ZAH-grehb

INTRODUCTION
WORDS IN A GRAPHIC WORLD

We live in a graphic world.

- When we see golden arches in any country, we know what's on the menu.
- The swoosh on a hat tells us what brand of shoe the athlete is wearing.
- A nose and mustache hanging from a pair of dark-rimmed glasses brings to mind only one comedian.
- A brown truck with a driver in a brown uniform announces the arrival of a package.
- Just three chime-like tones tell us which television network is tuned in.

Signature sounds convey a great deal in our culture. Color and shape communicate. The flourish of a graphic artist's pen captures the attention of casual viewers. A photographer's images move us to action. Is there still a place for words in a graphic world?

> **Have the emerging methods of communication made books obsolete?**

- We feel the exhilaration of war's end when the sailor kisses the woman in Times Square.
- We mourn as a three-year-old son mimics soldiers at his father's grave.
- We marvel as astronauts plant a flag on the surface of the moon.

- We pray as blindfolded hostages are paraded before the television cameras.

A picture is worth a thousand words. To tell the stories and describe the emotions evoked by just a single day's collection of images would tax even the most talkative person. Is there still a place for text in a photographic world?

Our methods of communication have changed dramatically in the past decade. Once a traveling businessman would write a letter to his wife; now it's a telephone call. Today's grandchild might find a letter in a shoe box; tomorrow's grandchild will never find a telephone call stuffed under a bed. E-mail has replaced snail-mail and is most often deleted after a short, digital life. Have the emerging methods of communication made books obsolete?

More importantly for those of us concerned about the good news of Jesus Christ, is there still a place for the written word in the work of the gospel?

This book, *Words of Life and Love,** shows us the importance of the print medium—how literature is being used to build the Kingdom around the world. Delve inside. Peruse the pages. Enter the graphic world of words.

---

*The title *Words of Life and Love* comes from the hymn "Father, Speak Your Word Again" (*Sing to the Lord*, No. 690) by Ken Bible.

1

SPRING UP, O WELL

Beneath the surface of eastern Australia lies an underground rock formation known as the Great Artesian Basin. Pressure builds as water trapped by the geological makeup of the region pushes to find an outlet. Sometimes a weakness in the earth's crust allows an artesian well to naturally bubble to the surface. Other times a rancher looking to provide water for his cattle or a farmer trying to irrigate his crops drills a well. They do not need a pump as the water rises on its own power.

In a similar fashion, World Mission Literature Ministries functions as a great artesian basin. The work of the World Mission Literature office in Kansas City operates largely unseen, like an aquifer buried deep in the earth. But go around the world to where Nazarenes use literature to share the Good News and you will find "a spring of water welling up to eternal life" (John 4:14). The local literature committee is the artesian well being fed by the World Mission Literature Ministries aquifer.

Snapshots of Literature Ministries

Market day in Papua New Guinea brings many people together. Some carry yams and taro to sell. A Bible school student stands at one end of the market with literature spread on a small table. People gather around the display to look at the books and hear the student explain the gospel message. In this marketplace the Bread of Life (John 6:35) is offered alongside the cassava.

A child in Hungary packs her bag as she prepares to leave the house for school. Among other items, she slips in a paper angel made at Sunday School. Later that day she tells the Christmas story as she holds high the paper angel as part of a show-and-tell presentation in her classroom. This school girl uses Sunday School literature to proclaim the good news that "a Savior has been born to you" (Luke 2:11).

Over a period of two months the pilot ferries more than 25,000 pieces of literature into Malawi to the great delight of national workers.

Key leaders from pastoral training centers in East Africa gather in Nairobi, Kenya, for a two-week, teach-the-teachers school. When the people return home, they carry with them additional books for the extension centers' libraries. Retired pastors and theological educators in the United States donate their personal libraries to World Mission Literature that in turn send the volumes to Africa. The books' journey ends in the 10 extension libraries in East Africa where 600 pastors will study to be able to correctly present the "word of truth" (2 Tim. 2:15).

A Nazarene Mission Aviation pilot checks the fluid levels in the engine of his plane, then completes the inspection of the aircraft for flight worthiness. Once again he heads for Malawi with discipleship materials for the five *JESUS* film teams in the

Writer's Conference in Africa

country. Over a period of two months the pilot ferries more than 25,000 pieces of literature into Malawi to the great delight of national workers. The pilot is a partner with the printer, and the literature writers are colleagues with the *JESUS* film evangelists in faithfully responding to God's command to "go and make disciples of all nations" (Matt. 28:19).

Some reports claimed that Amsterdam 2000 was more "international" than any other event in history, religious or secular. More than 10,000 Christian evangelists, including several from the Church of the Nazarene, represented 209 countries and territories. The conference featured about 900 seminars and services for training and worship. When the delegates from Thailand sang in the worship services, they used *Songs of Praise*, a hymnal produced by the Church of the Nazarene. Thai Christians joined their voices with believers from around the world to declare God's "glory among the nations" (Ps. 96:3).

The common denominator in each of these scenarios is World Mission Literature Ministries. In a sense, World Mission Literature functions as the publishing house for all non-English resources produced by the Church of the Nazarene. Unlike most publishers, however, World Mission Literature does not track inventory, schedule press runs, nor motivate a sales force. That is the domain of numerous literature committees working in more than 90 languages. (A list of these languages is located in the Appendix on page 79.) World Mission Literature Ministries supports the work of the individual literature committees by providing writer's conferences to train translators, writers, and editors; by coordinating the literature produced to avoid the duplication of effort; and by administering the funds used to produce and distribute the literature.

The Spanish Department Established

In the beginning days of world missions in the Church of the Nazarene, missionaries were responsible for providing all the literature they used in their work. If they needed a tract for evangelism, they would write the text, design the format, and print the literature. If they needed Sunday School curriculum or pastoral training materials, they would be author and publisher in addition to other responsibilities. Some missionaries had a mimeograph machine that they used to print literature for the church. Others had printing presses and trained available operators.

As the worldwide ministry of the Church of the Nazarene grew, it became increasingly evident that the publication of literature needed to be centralized to use resources and personnel efficiently. The growth of Spanish-language ministries, for example, both in the southern part of the United States and other countries, occurred so rapidly that missionaries and pastors could not keep up with the demand for literature. The 1944 General Assembly recognized this need of the growing church and authorized the formation of a new task force within the Department of Foreign Missions (now World Mission).

In the early summer of 1946, the Spanish Department came to life. Honorato Reza, a pastor, poet, and educator from Mexico, moved to Kansas City to serve as the editor of the new ministry. Moises Castillo from Puerto Rico was appointed to lead the production side of the enterprise. They went right to work. Three months after the staff arrived in Kansas City, the first issue of *El Heraldo de Santidad (Herald of Holiness)* came off of the press. Adult Sunday School curriculum soon followed. By 1949 Dr. Reza had developed a course of study for Spanish-speaking ministers and the process of providing textbooks was underway.

A Spanish radio broadcast, *La Hora Nazarena (Nazarene Hour)*, began production in 1953. For years every

> Within 20 years of the formation of the Spanish Department, the Church of the Nazarene became the second largest Protestant publisher of materials in Spanish.

broadcast featured one book from Casa Nazarena de Publicaciones (Nazarene Publishing House). The distribution system was so well developed that listeners could purchase the books at a local Christian bookstore. Within 20 years of the formation of the Spanish Department, the Church of the Nazarene became the second largest Protestant publisher of materials in Spanish. Nearly 200 titles had been printed—an amazing feat. The tremendous achievements of the Spanish Department were recorded in the 25th anniversary book and film, *A Cup of Warm Ink*, in 1971.

The increase of Churches of the Nazarene in Portuguese-speaking countries created the need for more coordination of Portuguese literature development. Consequently, church leaders moved the editorial office, originally located in Cape Verde, to Kansas City. The Spanish Department became the Latin Publications Division in 1971 with the additional responsibility for Portuguese literature.

The name changed again in 1976 with the creation of the International Publications Board as the church recognized the need for greater attention to the development of literature worldwide. Upon the recommendation of the General Board, the 1976 General Assembly added a paragraph (¶375) to the *Manual:* "There shall be an International Publications Board to coordinate and promote the preparation of printed publications, music, textbooks for educational institutions, and any other helps necessary for a distinctive church growth in Nazarene mission fields around the world."

The purpose as stated by the general assembly in 1976 remains intact today. The name has been modified a few times as adjustments have been made to create the most efficient administrative structure for the internationalization of the church. International Publications became Publications International, then World Literature Ministries, and eventually World Mission Literature Ministries. Through all of the name changes, however, the purpose remained the same. World Mission Literature Ministries coordinates the printing of non-English literature used to evangelize, disciple, and train.

Publishing Process

The publishing process begins and ends with one of the 65 literature committees. Most of the literature committees develop materials in one language for a localized region. Because of the number of people and countries for whom Spanish, Portuguese, or French is the primary language, literature development is more centralized for these languages.

As its first task, a literature committee must develop a strategy. Paramount to this process is the prioritization of the needs of the language group. The General Board approved a list of basic literature needs that form the foundation of a committee's strategy. These categories are the scriptures (see chap. 2); Sunday School curriculum (see chap. 3); a hymnal or songbook (see chap. 4); evangelism materials, literature that introduces the Church of the Nazarene, materials for denominational programs (Nazarene Missions International, Nazarene Youth

International, Sunday School Ministries), lay training materials, and ministerial training materials (see chap. 5); doctrinal books (see chap. 6); and the *Manual* of the Church of the Nazarene, either in part or in whole. A literature committee must assess the needs of pastors and laity that look to it for leadership, then create a publication agenda to address those needs in the most expedient manner.

While some Sunday School curricula and books are being written in Spanish, Portuguese, and Korean, most of the literature committees translate already published materials. Often this requires permission from the copyright owner to translate the original work. A literature committee, through the regional literature coordinator, sends a proposal to the World Mission Literature (WML) office that begins work on securing permission from the copyright holder.

After receiving a proposal, the personnel of WML begin the budgeting process. Most of the funds used for literature development come from the World Evangelism Fund. WML staff consider all the requests and include the dollar amount for literature in the World Mission Department budget that the General Board approves each year. A second source of funding for specific projects comes from individuals or congregations that donate money in memory of a person, congregations that adopt a project as part of their faith promise program, or children who raise money as part of a Vacation Bible School.

Once copyright permission is obtained and monies allocated, the literature committee can begin production.

Missionary Betty Sadat working with Pokomchi translators
in Guatemala, 1982

The translator serves as the most crucial person in the publication process. This individual must have excellent linguistic skills, a thorough understanding of the culture of the language group, and, for literature used in the work of ministry, a good grasp of biblical and theological principles. All three are necessary. To find a person who excels in all three areas is to discover a rare treasure. Sometimes a translator has the linguistic skill and cultural understanding but no training in the Bible or theology. To assist this person, the literature committee sometimes creates a lexicon of theological terms that articulates how specific concepts should be stated in the translation.

Computer programmers are working with linguists to develop software that translates documents from one language to another and back again. This endeavor is still in its infancy and does not yet provide much that benefits the work of World Mission

Literature. For example, in the middle of Mark 14 we find Jesus talking to Peter in the Garden of Gethsemane. Jesus prodded Peter with a question about his inability to watch and pray, then made the statement that "the spirit is willing, but the flesh is weak" (Mark 14:38, NASB). Using a computer program to translate from English to French, then back to English, the final result was "the spirit is laid out, but the flesh is weak." The attempt in Spanish concluded with the sentence "the alcohol is arranged, but the meat is weak." Until major advancement is made with linguistic computer programming, the church must continue to rely on human translators.

> **The church, once considered an enemy of the state, is now a trusted partner.**

Once the translator completes the basic translation, a series of steps to proof and edit the manuscript begins. Editors view the draft through three lenses—theological, cultural, and linguistic. The literature committee wants to insure that the truth of God is presented in a culturally appropriate manner with linguistic excellence. Even after a graphics artist has formatted the document for printing, the manuscript once again goes through a proof-and-edit cycle. Only after completing this rigorous review does the editor send the manuscript to the printer.

A literature committee sometimes forms its own publication company so it can legally operate in its country. Most church-related publishers, however, do not operate their own printing shops, but outsource to

Nazarene bookstore in Papua New Guinea

a local company the actual printing and binding of their literature. This often is the most cost-effective way to operate.

Once printed materials are ready, the literature committee manages their distribution. Some go to congregations to distribute without cost as they evangelize and disciple. Other items are sold, sometimes at a reduced rate, other times at full market value. Some of the books produced by the Church of the Nazarene are available at Christian bookstores in the region. In Eastern European countries, such as Hungary and Russia, the governments use Nazarene literature in the public school system. The church, once considered an enemy of the state, is now a trusted partner.

Missionary Daniel Psaute used literature extensively in his effort to plant the Church of the Nazarene in Croatia. In a letter to the World Mission Literature office, Daniel wrote, "There is almost no evangelical witness in the part of the city (Zagreb) where we live. We are making our presence known. Literature is essential to this process and to the establishment of our church."

A spring of water began to bubble in Croatia—just as it has in scores of countries. World Mission Literature Ministries is there, providing *words of life and love* to a dry land filled with thirsty people.

2

THE WORD
OF GOD

The Ethiopian eunuch did not find himself in this situation often. He needed help. Even the most casual observer saw that he was a man of wealth. Only a few could afford the luxury of the chariot in which he sat. He read from a personal copy of the Book of Isaiah; most people could not purchase a handwritten scroll. But this day his wealth provided little advantage.

On closer inspection an onlooker saw evidence of the Ethiopian's authority. If questioned, the Ethiopian would identify himself as a high-ranking governmental official. He managed the financial affairs of the nation for Candace, the queen of Ethiopia. His authority failed him, though, as he contemplated the words of the prophet Isaiah.

Persecution in Jerusalem scattered the disciples of Jesus in every direction. Philip shared the Good News convincingly in Samaria, and the revival brought great joy to the region. But God needed Philip in another place and pointed him toward the desert. Without hesitation Philip headed south. If he had delayed, he might have missed the Ethiopian on his way home.

As Philip approached the Ethiopian's chariot,

he heard the man reading from Isaiah 53. The Ethiopian had all kinds of questions for Philip. Was Isaiah talking about himself? Or was there someone else?

The Ethiopian eagerly listened as Philip talked about Jesus. After hearing the *words of life and love*, the Ethiopian eunuch acknowledged Jesus as the Anointed One of God. With great rejoicing Philip baptized the Ethiopian before this new disciple set out to carry the Good News to Africa.

Making the Scripture Available

The Church of the Nazarene believes that God has revealed in the Bible everything we need to know for salvation and holy living. Our doctrine emerges from the systematic study of the Scriptures. We build our lifestyle on biblical principles. The Bible is the final authority for all aspects of our understanding of God and our relationship with the Savior.

The Bible in the language of the people, then, sits at top of the list of literature needs in the work of the Church of the Nazarene. Because Bible translation is such a specialized process, we often rely on the work of Bible societies. There have been a few instances, however, when Nazarenes have done the hard work of Bible translation.

Making the Bible accessible through studies and lessons has been and will always be a major undertaking for World Mission Literature. Just as Philip helped the Ethiopian to understand what he read, so literature committees work to make the scriptures available to the people wanting to know the Word of God.

Gospel of John in K'ekchí

When missionary William Sadat went to live in Guatemala, there were 300,000 K'ekchí Indians without a Bible in their language. So he began translating the Gospel of John. Surrounded by reference books, William discussed with K'ekchí assistants the best way to translate God's Word so that it remained true to the original languages yet understandable by the people in northern Guatemala. Sometimes only a few verses would be completed at the end of a day. But the translation team persisted—word by word, phrase by phrase, verse by verse.

The first press run of the K'ekchí edition of John's Gospel was printed on the Nazarene Printing Press in Cobán, Guatemala. The 1,000 initial copies soon sold out. The American Bible Society recognized the importance of Sadat's work and printed the Gospel of Mark when William completed it a few years later. The translation work started by a Nazarene missionary took on larger proportions.

In 1955 the Guatemala government acknowledged the work of William and his wife, Betty, when it printed the first K'ekchí-Spanish dictionary, a book developed during their translation of the New Testament into K'ekchí.

The complete K'ekchí New Testament was officially presented to the K'ekchí people on Sunday, August 20, 1961. About 1,300 people gathered to celebrate. Tributes were spoken to William and Betty Sadat and the Indian helpers who worked with them. The sweetest words, however, came from a little Indian woman when she said, "When I read those

Missionary William Sadat presenting the K'ekchí New Testament
to Nazarenes in Guatemala, 1961

words in my own language, it seems to me that Jesus
lives in our village."[1]

Literacy in Papua New Guinea

How do you provide the Scriptures to people
for whom the printed page is merely undecipherable
lines and dots? No matter how long they stare at the
page, no discernable pattern emerges. Missionaries
working in the highlands of Papua New Guinea face
such a challenge.

The government of Papua New Guinea (PNG)

defines literacy as the "ability to write a paragraph about an identifiable object in an individual's vernacular language."[2] Using this definition, about 70 percent of the New Guineans in the urban areas are literate, but only about 22 percent of those living in rural areas can read and write. Only about 5 percent of school-aged children in PNG complete grade 10.

Not only are many New Guineans unable to read the books used by the missionaries, they have a learning style that greatly differs from that of the missionaries. The people of PNG learn in a way similar to that of Old Testament Hebrews—through stories, symbols, and ritual. Missionaries trained in Western culture most likely attended schools more in line with the Hellenistic practice of New Testament times—a logical, reasoned approach to learning.

> The people of PNG learn in a way similar to that of Old Testament Hebrews—through stories, symbols, and ritual.

The challenge for church leaders, then, is to provide the Word of God to people who, at best, have limited reading skills and learn most effectively through graphic methods.

Stick Figure Pictures

In the 1960s several Christian mission agencies working in Papua New Guinea began experimenting with drawings of stick figures to tell Bible stories. Nazarene missionary Neville Bartle sent a delegation of local church leaders to a Bible conference where the stick figures formed the primary teaching method. In spite of their illiteracy, the men returned home after gaining more Bible knowledge in one week than they had learned in all the years they had been Christians. With great enthusiasm the men showed Neville the charts they brought home.

Neville immediately saw the charts as a perfect tool to use in PNG. Instead of words, there were stick figures, so illiterate people would have access to God's Word. The stick figures were graphic, something that fit the natural learning style of the New Guinean. With more than 800 languages in the country of about 5 million people, one stick figure chart could travel from village to village, still effective in spite of a change of dialect.

Over time missionary Bartle refined the process to maximize the effectiveness of using stick figures to teach the Bible.

Wanting to capitalize on the method, Neville started drawing Bible stories on a flip chart about two feet wide and three feet high. He divided each flip chart page into nine sections like a giant ticktacktoe game with a portion of the Bible story drawn in each section. Once Neville completed the master flip chart, he mounted it on a sheet of glass. With the glass positioned to maximize the benefit of sunlight, a Bible school student traced the drawings on a second sheet to make another flip chart. And another. And another.

Once about a dozen charts were ready, leaders from surrounding congregations came together for a training session. Neville taught the Bible lesson using the stick figure charts. The leaders then formed small groups to discuss the lesson and practice teaching it themselves. A final session allowed Neville to answer questions raised during the small-group meetings. The leaders left the training with a copy of the flip charts under their arms, ready to spread the Word. The lesson they learned on Friday would be taught on Sunday in their local churches, then repeated in house meetings through the week.

Neville traveled to the villages to observe how the flip charts were being used. He observed the responses of the people and listened to the types of questions they asked. This information prompted

Bible school students in Papua New Guinea drawing flip charts

Flip charts mounted on glass for tracing

adjustments in the process when he returned home to begin work on the next set of Bible stories. Over time missionary Bartle refined the process to maximize the effectiveness of using stick figures to teach the Bible.

The positive impact of the new teaching method quickly became evident. The people's understanding of the Word of God grew, and their spiritual lives deepened. The songs the New Guinean Christians composed and sang in worship services took on a more profound character as they understood more fully God's design for the spiritual life.

Church leaders wanted to expand the availability

of the flip charts and became frustrated with the laborious methods for reproducing them. The tracing process took a great deal of time, and the quality was often poor. In 1994 Jim Wiesen, a retired graphic artist from the United States, went to Papua New Guinea to upgrade the production methods. When Jim visited PNG on an earlier Work and Witness team, he saw the effectiveness of the stick figure Bible lessons and the inadequate production methods. He offered his skill as an artist to help the church in PNG become more efficient in the work of ministry.

Jim's contribution began as he redrew the stick figures to show movement and expression. Then he helped set up a silk screen printing press. The tedious task of tracing the stick figures was replaced with a process that could produce as many as 150 charts in one afternoon. Not only the quantity but the quality of the charts improved dramatically.

Eventually Jim scanned the pictures so they can be stored on a computer disk. About 2,000 line drawings are now available for use in a variety of formats.

In addition to flip charts, mission staff also printed chart books. Instead of nine pictures on a flip chart, a page in the chart book has only one picture. The facing page of the book included the Bible story with commentary in Pidgin English, the trade language of PNG. A person able to read could tell the Bible story as a person unable to read looked at the stick figure pictures. These Bible story books have been revised, expanded, and reprinted over the years.

World Mission Literature (WML) Ministries that made these publications possible in Papua New

Guinea administered the monies for literature from the World Evangelism Fund. More important, WML assists the people involved with literature development in PNG. The literature coordinator for the Asia-Pacific Region gives general oversight. The literature committee chair for the Melanesia Field—Papua New Guinea, Solomon Islands, East Timor, and Vanuatu—leads the program to develop resources designed specifically for the region. Local persons are being trained, from writers to printing press operators. At each level—region, field, and local—World Mission Literature Ministries supports the work of the gospel.

A Women's Conference

More than 1,000 women from various parts of Papua New Guinea were expected to attend a Bible conference. The organizers wanted the Bible lessons to be transferable. They desired that those who attended the conference take the life and love found in God's Word with them to their homes.

The conference organizers called Bible teachers to gather for training. This was the first step of the strategy to distribute the Word of God to those who need to hear the truth. First the teachers must be learners. Thirty women sat on narrow wooden benches in a village church with woven bamboo walls, a concrete floor, and a corrugated metal roof. The main teacher held an open Bible in

> The sounds of several vernacular languages rang through the church as the women prepared to teach.

one hand and a pointing stick in the other. As she told the Bible story, she pointed to pictures of stick figures on the flip chart beside her. When a learner had a question, she responded with an answer from God's Word.

After the initial training session, the 30 women divided into groups of 2 or 3 to practice teaching the lesson. The sounds of several vernacular languages rang through the church as the women prepared to teach. Each woman had a small version of the stick figure chart. The groups studied the pictures, discussed the meaning of the text, and rehearsed the story again and again.

When the women again gathered in one group, the leader asked them to share insights that came as they met in small groups. Questions were answered. A prayer for God's blessing concluded the training.

When the women's conference convened, these 30 teachers used stick figure flip charts to tell the story of Jesus, the light of the world. The flame that passed from one leader to 30 teachers was passed to 1,000 women who in turn carried it to their villages to share with others. The Word of God is a light for the mountain paths of Papua New Guinea.

———
1. Lorraine O. Schultz, *Bringing God's Word to Guatemala: The Life and Work of William and Betty Sadat* (Kansas City: Nazarene Publishing House, 1995), 56.
2. Doug Flemming, "PNG Literacy," *Imprint*, January/February 2001, 3.

3

WORDS OF
SPIRITUAL NURTURE

Weeds filled the mission field in which the apostle Paul labored. In Galatia Paul pulled the weed of legalism that was choking the flower of freedom in Christ. In Philippi he whacked at envy and rivalry to give the joy of the Lord a chance to blossom. In Colosse Paul battled all that would encroach on the supremacy of Christ. His written words were the tools used to remove weeds from the garden of God.

No place brought on the hay fever for Paul like Corinth. Weeds were in full bloom in that city. For 18 months Paul tended the garden in Corinth, yet three years later the weeds had overrun the clearing again. Paul sent Timothy, then Titus, to join the battle. Finally Paul wrote a letter "to warn you, as my dear children" (1 Cor. 4:14). They needed instruction from their spiritual father.

Paul lived with the believers at Thessalonica to teach them about God's call to holy living. The lessons sent roots down deep. Later Paul wrote to encourage them to continue growing in holiness. The love of God in their hearts had produced the fruit of love for each other. Paul wrote to urge them "to do so more and more" (1 Thess. 4:10). He nurtured the young plants through his writings.

In our day, too, we need words of spiritual nurture. Sometimes we need the protection that words of warning provide. Other times we need spiritual nourishment provided by a study of God's Word. Anywhere in the world, Sunday School often serves as the means through which disciples of Christ "grow in the grace and knowledge of our Lord and Savior Jesus Christ" (2 Pet. 3:18).

Hectographs and Mimeographs

Before the existence of World Mission Literature Ministries and its predecessors, individual missionaries were responsible for all literature needs in their region. They might find books printed by other Christian groups that they could use as long as they were compatible with the doctrine of the Church of the Nazarene. Missionaries often looked for new literature while on furlough. After transporting the collected editions to the mission field, they then translated and printed the literature for use in their ministry.

Compared with today's technology, the printing process was often quite primitive. Some missionaries used a hectograph. Using a pan similar to one in which a cake is baked, they poured a liquid solution into the pan and allowed it to jell. They utilized a special ink to type the text and draw the graphics as they prepared the master page. Laying the master face-down on the gelatinous material, they were able to transfer the image to the printing surface. Now they were ready to print. They placed blank sheets on the gelatin printing surface, then lifted the paper and allowed it to dry. Even though the prefix *hecto-* in hectograph means 100, often people could print no more than 50 copies at one time using this method.

Other missionaries used a mimeograph machine. Using a typewriter and stylus, people prepared a stencil and wrapped it tightly but smoothly on a cylinder. As the cylinder rotated—early machines by a hand crank—a pressure roller forced ink through the cutouts in the stencil and onto the paper.

Operating a hectograph would turn your fingers purple. The black ink of a mimeograph could be quite messy as well.

Soon after missionaries Spurgeon and Fae Hendrix arrived in Argentina in 1940, the Argentine leaders decided to print tracts for evangelistic work.

Printing Sunday School lessons in the Pokomchi language
by mimeograph, circa 1980

A student at the Bible school had a little experience with the printing process, so he became the first press operator. Mission officials purchased a small printing press and converted the garage of the house where the Hendrix family lived into a press room. Soon the Argentine Nazarenes had Christian literature to share with neighbors and friends.

Sunday School literature was scarce in the early 1940s in Argentina. Fae translated children's Christian education materials for use in Nazarene congregations. Others translated Christian Service Training (CST) books, and Argentine leaders almost made it mandatory that every Sunday School teacher complete the three levels of training. Since the future of the church depends on making disciples, missionaries gave their best effort to the ministry of nurture.

In 1940 a printing press in a garage supplied Nazarene congregations in Argentina with the literature they needed. Effectiveness and efficiency have greatly increased now that World Mission Literature Ministries guides the development of materials used throughout the Spanish-speaking world.

Sunday School Curriculum in Hungary

Prior to the beginning of the Church of the Nazarene in Hungary in 1996, Christian churches in that country sponsored Sunday Schools, but they

> Since the future of the church depends on making disciples, missionaries gave their best effort to the ministry of nurture.

Literature committee in Hungary

were not a priority. Sunday School (SS) teachers received no training. If a teacher had exceptional natural ability, then the SS class would flourish. Most of the time, however, Sunday School languished in Hungarian congregations.

During this time SS teachers had to create most of the resources they used with the children under their care. Only a small selection of SS literature could be purchased, and that was of poor quality. A few congregations owned a flannelgraph set provided by people in the United States, but not much else existed.

With no list of suggested topics, a SS teacher would develop a new lesson each week. The teacher often relied on a limited repertoire of teaching methods. Sometimes the learning activities were not appropriate for the age and developmental level of the students.

Imre and Mária Gusztin returned to Hungary in 1996 after studying at European Nazarene College in Büsingen, Switzerland. They went right to work to plant the Church of the Nazarene. By the end of 1998 they had established four congregations. The leaders of these congregations recognized immediately they needed help with children's ministries, so the Gusztins organized a meeting for all children's workers in the four congregations. The participants mentioned the need for Hungarian resources available for children's ministry. They shared teaching ideas with each other. While their time together benefited all persons present, a sense of melancholy pervaded the gathering when they realized that the resources they really needed were not available.

Imre showed the group WordAction Sunday School curriculum from the Nazarene Publishing House. While a student at European Nazarene College, Imre worked in the library. One time he asked for permission to take outdated curriculum destined to be discarded. When the Gusztins returned to Hungary, they decided to leave a couple of furniture items behind so they could take the WordAction curriculum with them.

Imre had taught classes in English using the WordAction curriculum. He knew firsthand of its effectiveness. As he showed the children's ministry leaders from the emerging Hungarian church the literature available in English, the emotional tone in the room turned noticeably brighter. The children's workers immediately began to brainstorm about how they could use the English material in Hungarian Sunday Schools.

Since many of those who served in children's ministry did not read English, curriculum writers prepared teaching instructions in Hungarian and added captions for the pictures in the resource packets. As the teachers tried the new material, their responses were enthusiastic.

A larger vision began to come into focus, a dream that included excellent SS literature to match the 99 percent literacy rate in Hungary. What if they used the format and graphics from the WordAction curriculum and translated the text? They made the decision to give it a try. In one month a group of dedicated volunteers prepared four lessons to be used to tell the Christmas story during the month of December. They translated and edited. They used their own computers and printers. Then 240 hours later Hungarian Nazarenes joyfully looked at the top-notch Sunday School literature they produced. A new ministry was born.

> Hungarian Nazarenes joyfully looked at the top-notch Sunday School literature they produced. A new ministry was born.

As the trial expanded with more SS materials produced, the ardent response overwhelmed the literature committee. Children excitedly told their friends about Sunday School as they showed them the activity sheets. Parents heard about the SS, dis-

**Literature committee in Hungary demonstrating
WordAction to church leaders**

covered the time and location, and brought their
children. Since most individuals in Hungary do not
own cars and public transportation is not readily
available, some parents walked several kilometers
with their children, waited until the SS session
ended, then returned home. Other parents knocked
on the door of the house where the SS session was
being held, asking if their children could participate.
Grandparents brought grandchildren. Largely due to
the quality of the curriculum, Nazarene Sunday
School in Hungary grew from 1 teacher with 2 children in a single congregation in 1997 to 10 teachers

with 70 children in 4 congregations in the year 2000.

The SS teachers were energized too. No longer did they need to select a topic each week or create learning activities. Now they had clearly defined objectives for each lesson with age-appropriate teaching methods. Each lesson built on the previous ones to form cohesive units. Over time the units provided a balanced plan of spiritual instruction for the children.

When the personnel of World Mission Literature heard what was developing in Hungary, they immediately saw the global impact of the methods the Hungarian literature committee created. What if the WordAction curriculum, a product developed with the best of biblical scholarship and educational principles, could be made available to literature committees around the world? Instead of each literature committee starting from scratch, they would begin with what had been developed and adapt it to the needs of congregations in their region.

World Mission Literature alerted Sunday School leaders at the international headquarters in Kansas City and administrators at Nazarene Publishing House about the work of the Hungarian literature committee. Key leaders went to Hungary to see first hand what they were doing. On February 25, 2000, three members of the Hungarian literature committee met in Kansas City with representatives of World Mission Literature, Sunday School Ministries, Word-Action, and Nazarene Publishing House to explore expansion of the Hungarian project.

Over the next several months they refined the process and rewrote the operations manual. World

Mission Literature took the lead in finding the funding for this creative initiative. They purchased new equipment to fully utilize what Nazarene Publishing House provided.

In September 2001 the Hungarian WordAction curriculum committee began to implement the newly developed plan. They placed the first order for resource material from the Nazarene Publishing House (NPH). Under the agreement, NPH supplies the Hungarian literature committee SS curriculum on CD-ROM, a digital storage format that can be used on a computer. Included on the CD-ROM are all the text and graphics needed to print the literature. Once the Hungarian literature committee receives the CD-ROM, a person translates all text from English to Hungarian. A language editor revises the translation, then sends it to production. Using the graphics and layout of the original WordAction materials, the Hungarian translation replaces English text. The final step in the process involves taking the computer files to a commercial printer for printing and binding. When the Sunday School pieces are printed, they look just like the English version except for the Hungarian text.

The literature committee looks carefully at the WordAction materials for cultural appropriateness for the Hungarian people. The committee sometimes approves a graphic even though children in their country may not understand a football helmet on a stuffed bear in an illustration. Occasionally the group decides to insert a new graphic. They may rewrite a story with an automobile as a central part, since the family of a Hun-

What started out as an attempt to meet the need of four Nazarene congregations for quality SS material is becoming an international phenomenon.

garian child likely does not own a car, or they may change references to foods not found in Hungary, such as peanut butter. For the most part, however, the Hungarian literature committee uses the English text "as is" in its translation work.

With the availability of the new curriculum, church leaders hold SS teacher training conferences to show the eager Christian educators how to increase their effectiveness. Other denominations have shown great interest in what the Church of the Nazarene is producing. The Wesleyan Alliance, a consortium of six denominations and mission agencies who trace their heritage to John Wesley, will utilize the product. As news of this material has spread throughout Hungary, even some civic leaders have expressed an interest in purchasing the curriculum for use in public schools. The literature may also reach Hungarian congregations in Romania, Slovakia, Serbia, Ukraine, and Croatia. What started out as an attempt to meet the need of four Nazarene congregations for quality SS material is becoming an international phenomenon.

Nazarene literature committees in other parts of the world are eagerly cheering the Hungarian team. If this experiment proves to be as successful as it appears early in the process, then other literature committees will quickly devise plans to utilize the methods developed in Hungary.

The strategy of the Hungarian literature committee begins with children's literature and gradually adds age levels until a fully graded SS curriculum is available. The Hungarian leaders work today with its vision focused 20 years in the future. That will be the time when children using the literature begin to take places of leadership in the church. The church of tomorrow will be strong because children heard words of spiritual nurture today.

Hungarian Wesleyan Alliance

4

WORDS OF
WORSHIP

The glazed tiles that covered the walls and gates shimmered in the sunlight. In the middle of the desert, lush gardens levitated up to 75 feet above the ground. A 300-foot tower reached to the heavens as part of the Temple of Marduk complex. Babylonians thought they lived in the center of the world, maybe the universe.

The river Euphrates ran along the western wall of Babylon with canals branching off into various parts of the city. Beside the water sat a dejected man. A musician, his harp hung in a nearby tree, unused. Some who happened to walk by saw that the man was not only a musician, but one of the captives from Jerusalem. "Sing us one of the songs of Zion!" they demanded (Ps. 137:3). The musician didn't even look up. One of the tormentors tossed out a caustic remark to the amusement of his friends, who then walked away, leaving the musician to himself.

"How rude," he mumbled, "wanting to be entertained by the songs intended to be sung to God." The songs he learned in the Jerusalem Temple seemed out of place in Babylon. But what does a person sing "in a foreign land"? (Ps. 137:4).

Missionaries in the 21st century ask the same question. Hymns that speak of being whiter than snow lose significance for a congregation in a tropical rain forest. To testify that Jesus lives in your heart may mystify the person in a culture where the bowels or throats are considered the core of a person's being. Songs appropriate for Christian worship created by indigenous people may be few. So what do congregations sing in worship?

A Variety of Hymnals

During the first several decades in the history of the Church of the Nazarene, missionaries and local leaders were solely responsible for the literature they needed in their ministries. Visible only in retrospect, things began to change dramatically in 1943 with the formation of a committee to produce a hymnal that could be used in all Spanish-speaking countries.

The Spanish Department, the predecessor of World Mission Literature Ministries, "grew out of the original [Spanish] hymnal committee."[1] After the committee completed its work, the members began to discuss other Spanish literature needs. In January 1944 the Department of Foreign Missions (now World Mission) considered the formation of a permanent commission to prepare, publish, and distribute liter-

From Afrikaans to Zulu in Africa, from Burmese to Waray-Waray (Philippines) in Asia-Pacific, the Church of the Nazarene has produced almost 60 hymnals in the last 50 years.

49

ature for use in Spanish-language countries. The general assembly meeting in Minneapolis in 1944 finalized the plan with the creation of the Spanish Department. The work of World Mission Literature today traces its heritage back to a Spanish hymnal committee.

From Afrikaans to Zulu in Africa, from Burmese to Waray-Waray (Philippines) in Asia-Pacific, the Church of the Nazarene has produced almost 60 hymnals in the last 50 years. World Mission Literature Ministries assists with the publication of books for congregational singing.

About three-quarters of the hymnals printed in the last 50 years are words-only editions. A few list the hymnal or songbook where the users can locate the music. For example, *Tinsimu ta Kutwanana*, the 1956 hymnal in Shangaan (Africa), lists 23 books as the music sources of the hymn texts in the volume. *Nazarene Kohhran Hla Bu*, the 1987 Burmese hymnal, provided the tonal center of the tune, for example, "do is G" or "do is E." Some of the hymns in books from the Philippines include the time signature and whether the first note is on the downbeat or a pickup note. For the most part, however, a words-only hymnal provides no indication of the hymn tune. Most of the time the use of this type of hymnal requires the congregation to simply know the tune from memory.

Missionaries used a typewriter and mimeograph machine to produce some of the words-only hymnals printed 50 years ago. Stapling a simple paper cover over a few pages, they created the songbook. In recent years mission personnel have typeset hymnals using a computer before sending the computer files to a commercial printer for printing and binding. The Thai hymnal published in 1999 used this method.

Songs of Praise: A Christian Hymnal for Worship

Nazarene missionaries in Thailand recognized a great need to provide resources that would improve congregational singing. Only two Thai hymnals, more than 40 years old, were available. Neither one of these hymnals included songs from the Wesleyan/Holiness Movement. A few words-only songbooks were in circulation, but they contained many errors.

> The task to select hymns and songs can be daunting.

Missionaries set out to remedy the situation. Editing a hymnal requires musical skill that many missionaries do not possess, but the Church of the Nazarene had people in Thailand trained and ready for the task. By 1995 they had produced a prototype hymnal with about 200 songs. With photocopies in hand, they began to discuss with other Christian organizations the possibility of producing a Thai hymnal. The Thailand Baptist Churches Association had funds already designated for a hymnal, but they didn't have anyone with the necessary musical expertise to head up the project. The Nazarenes and Baptists then formed a partnership.

Work on the Thai hymnal began in earnest in 1996. The task at hand was to produce a songbook that included the hymns from the past, the worship songs from the present, and new compositions by Thai Christians. Using the organizational structure of *Sing to the Lord*, the 1993 English hymnal of the Church of the Nazarene, missionary personnel began to develop *Songs of Praise*.

The task to select hymns and songs can be daunting. A literature committee may consider more than twice the number of hymns included in the final collection; therefore, they must make some hard decisions. For the sake of keeping the thematic sections of a hymnal in proportion, the committee may omit some good songs in favor of others that will balance the collection. In the case of the Thai hymnal, a committee of Christians from various organizations sorted through nearly 600 hymns. In the

Sample pages from the Thai hymnal

end, the group selected 422 for publication in the Thai hymnal.

Missiologists today debate the appropriateness of using Western music in a non-Western culture. Christians trained in the field of ethnomusicology, the study of music in culture, encourage the creation of Scripture songs in the traditional musical language of a people using familiar musical instruments. This effort provides Christians expressions of their faith in their "heart language."

The Thai hymnal selection committee considered several songs written by Christians in the traditional Thai musical style. Since the complexity of this style makes it difficult for a congregation to sing together, the committee rejected all such songs under consideration while including some songs written by Thai Christians in a contemporary Western style.

When hymnals are not available to people in a country or region, congregational songs are often learned by hearing them sung. People may hear Christian songs while visiting other churches, then later teach them to their congregations. If this has been the practice, hymnal compilers often discover several versions of one particular song. The music and text are altered as the song passes from person to person, congregation to congregation, until at the end of the chain the words and/or tune is quite different from the original. This process is similar to the party game where a whispered message passes from person to person before the whole group compares the original and final messages. What is a source of laughter at a party can make the hymnal compiler's task diffi-

> A word-for-word translation of a hymn rarely is possible.

cult. Which is the correct version of the song?

When the Church of the Nazarene began compiling the Russian-language hymnal published in 2000, they discovered several versions of some hymns. While the Russians lived under Communism for 70 years, free communication between believers did not exist in the vast realm of the former Soviet Union. One translator did not know that another translator had prepared a hymn text in Russian. When religious fetters were removed, Russian Christians started learning more

Copies of the Thai and Russian hymnals

about the songs other believers sang in worship. The Russian hymnal committee had to choose between various versions of one hymn. Sometimes they decided to include two versions of the same song on adjoining pages of the hymnal.

The translator of a hymn text must be as much a poet as the creator of the original. A word-for-word translation of a hymn rarely is possible. Metaphors and other figures of speech from one language may be meaningless in another culture, so the translator will search for an appropriate substitute.

The accents of the text must match the accents of the music. The natural accents of a melody written for an English text are crucial factors when translating the text into another language. The Thai language adds another dilemma for the hymn translator in that the language is tonal. In addition to vowels and consonants, five tones—high, mid, low, rising, and falling—determine the meaning of words. The translator of a hymn attempts to find words that have high tones to go with the higher notes of a melody, and words with low tones to go with the lower notes. This makes the process of translating hymns quite challenging.

Securing copyright permission to print hymns and songs is a gargantuan task. For the Thai hymnal, the literature committee contacted about 35 copyright owners in eight countries, including Germany, England, the United States, Australia, New Zealand, and Singapore. Some allow the use of their songs without charge. Others refuse to grant permission under any condition. Some want to review the trans-

A worship
leader in
Thailand us-
ing *Songs of
Praise* has
every re-
source that
is available
to a worship
leader in the
United
States using
*Sing to the
Lord*.

lation prior to issuing a contract. Almost every copyright owner wants one
or two review copies once the hymnal
is printed.

Finale® software allows the user to
print music using a computer. With an
electronic music keyboard attached to
a computer, the operator depresses
keys on the music keyboard to assign
pitches and note values to the music
score displayed on the computer moni-
tor. Once the person enters the music,
he or she assigns the hymn text to
notes syllable by syllable. Nazarene
missionaries used this method to "en-
grave" the Thai hymnal. Since guitar
players are often more available than
pianists, in many current hymnals
chord symbols are included above the treble staff.
Once missionaries prepared the master copies of the
Thai hymnal, a commercial printer printed and
bound the hymnals.

A Nazarene missionary also prepared a *Resource
Manual* for the Thai hymnal. Much like *Resources for
Worship Planning: A Companion to the Hymnal Sing
to the Lord*, the Thai book includes a variety of tools
a leader can use in the worship planning process.
Chapter 1 discusses the nature of worship. Chapter
2 outlines various ways a worship planner can fully
utilize the hymnal. Subsequent chapters provide
various indices, Scripture references in hymns, and
helps for modulating from one key to another. A

worship leader in Thailand using *Songs of Praise* has every resource that is available to a worship leader using the English version of *Sing to the Lord*.

Many Christian congregations in Thailand are now using *Songs of Praise*. In addition to being available from the Church of the Nazarene and the Thailand Baptist Churches Association, the two official sponsors of the volume, Christians can purchase the hymnal in bookstores throughout the country. Christian leaders selected this hymnal as the official hymnbook for the Thai delegation to Amsterdam 2000, the worldwide gathering of evangelists sponsored by the Billy Graham Evangelistic Association.

The effort of missionaries to enhance worship in Churches of the Nazarene in Thailand has resulted in the strengthening of the larger Body of Christ in that country. We rejoice that the ministry of World Mission Literature often reaches beyond denominational lines to serve all Christians who follow our Lord and Savior—providing *words of life and love* through music.

------

1. Franklin Cook, *A Cup of Warm Ink* (Kansas City: Nazarene Publishing House, 1971), 18.

5

Words to Equip

In true Johnny Appleseed fashion, the apostle Paul traveled throughout the Roman Empire scattering the seeds of the gospel. When a seed germinated and sent up a sprout, Paul nurtured and cultivated the young plant. Sometimes Paul spent months in a city, discipling the young Christians and training leaders for the new congregation. Other times he followed the leading of the Spirit and moved on after a few days. Occasionally Paul sent someone like Timothy or Titus to provide pastoral leadership for a growing congregation.

Paul lived in Ephesus for almost three years, serving the congregation as its first pastor. Sometime later, after false teachers attempted to dilute the gospel with myths, Paul commissioned Timothy as the Ephesian pastor. Being a timid fellow, Timothy needed encouragement to stay with the task. Paul said, "I am writing you these instructions so that . . . you will know how people ought to conduct themselves in God's household" (1 Tim. 3:14-15). Paul equipped Pastor Timothy who in turn equipped "God's people for works of service, so that the body of Christ may be built up" (Eph. 4:12).

Out of all the ministry resources available to the Church of the Nazarene, the human resources prove the most valuable. Just as God sent the gospel in human form when Jesus came to earth, so God continues to spread the Good News person by person. This requires placing the training of pastors near the top of the priority list. Paul trained Timothy to be a pastor, and the Church of the Nazarene trains ministers of the gospel to nurture and nourish the disciples of Jesus.

Schools for Pastoral Training

The International Board of Education of the Church of the Nazarene facilitates the work of 46 seminaries, universities, colleges, and Bible institutes involved in training Nazarene pastors outside of the United States and Canada. In addition to the formal schools, centers for Theological Education by Extension provide instruction for more than 10,000 persons unable to enroll in a traditional program. Whether a university with a sizable campus or an extension center hosted by a local church, the teachers and students need books in the learning process.

As a school develops degree programs, it becomes necessary to seek accreditation from the appropriate agency. Through the accreditation process the school demonstrates to an accreditation team that it offers a quality education. Accreditation is a seal of approval that has great importance in the educational community. For example, three organizations—the Asia Theological Association, the Association of Theological Educa-

> Accreditation is a seal of approval that has great importance in the educational community.

tion for South East Asia, and the Philippine Association of Bible and Theological Schools—have fully accredited Asia-Pacific Nazarene Theological Seminary (APNTS). In addition, APNTS, located in a suburb of Manila, has government recognition from the Commission on Higher Education, Republic of the Philippines. These various agencies validate the quality of education available at APNTS.

An accreditation team will carefully examine the library resources available to students at the school. If the school's library does not provide adequate resources, the accreditation team will note that in its report, and sometimes will direct the school to address the deficiency before the accreditation process can proceed.

When the Caribbean Nazarene Theological College (CNTC) first applied for accreditation, the accreditation team found inadequacies in the library. Two librarians from the United States, Maurine Dickerson and Pat Westmoreland, went to Trinidad twice for three-month work periods in which they revised the catalog system for the 10,000-volume library. When these dedicated volunteers completed the massive task, the library offered a much better learning environment to the students. CNTC received the accreditation it sought.

Books in Mission

The CNTC library benefited in another way. Over the years the Books in Mission program of World Mission Literature Ministries has sent more than 3,000 used books to Trinidad. The study op-

Dr. Bennett Dudney

tions available to ministerial students increased with these additions to the library.

Books in Mission is a program begun in 1986 to send used or surplus literature to schools outside the United States and Canada. Since Nazarene schools in many parts of the world teach in English, the books have an eager audience. Dr. Bennett Dudney, then director of WML, used his leadership skills to make his long-time dream, Books in Mission, a reality.

Donations of used books for pastoral training

come from many sources. Retired pastors and missionaries are a prime source, as are educators. Duplicate books in church libraries, or those not used recently, can find a place of active service in a Bible college library. Congregations and senior adult groups have caught the vision and gathered used books. At the 2001 General Assembly in Indianapolis, interested people dropped off 1,079 books at the World Mission Literature exhibit for the Books in Mission (BIM) program.

When donated books arrive at the offices of World Mission Literature in Kansas City, they find their way to a processing room in the lower level of the Administration Center. The BIM coordinator enters the book title, author, and subject category in a computer database before shelving the book according to subject.

Books in Mission workers circulate the database printout among schools that prepare Nazarene pastors. A school librarian, professor, or administrator goes through the list, selecting those books that will fill gaps in the school's current collection. Used books are available from World Mission Literature on a first-come, first-served basis, so a prompt reply on the part of the school is advantageous.

BIM personnel prepare the books for the school that requested them, sending them in mail bags, sometimes dozens of boxes and hundreds of books at a time. The receiving school library pays the postage out of its literature budget, but the total expenditure is much less than it would be if the library purchased the books at a retail or even wholesale outlet.

Processing area for the Books in Mission program

Responding to a Need

While teaching at the Asia-Pacific Nazarene Theological Seminary for a semester in 1998 and again in 2000, Wesley Tracy and his wife, Bettye, had opportunity to teach workshops at two other schools in the Philippines: Luzon Nazarene Bible College and Visayan Nazarene Bible College. Some who attended the workshop at Visayan traveled 15 hours by boat and bus. Sessions went from nine in the morning to nine at night, the learners craving knowledge, and Wes and Bettye relying on strength from the Lord to keep up. When Dr. Tracy saw the meager library resources available to eager students, he immediately determined to donate his personal library to those schools upon his retirement. He saw a need and recognized that God had already supplied the answer through his donation of more than 1,000 books.

In 1999 Al Truesdale visited Africa Nazarene University (ANU) to advise Vice Chancellor Leah Marangu on the needs in the religion department. As part of his visit, Dr. Truesdale talked with the librarian. He noted that the library did not have many of the most current books in the subjects of theology and philosophy. When he retired as a professor at Nazarene Theological Seminary, Dr. Truesdale packed up almost 1,200 books and donated them to Books in Mission. At his direction, BIM sent the whole collection to ANU.

Alpin Bowes taught an adult Sunday School class for 36 years in addition to his service to the Church of the Nazarene as a pastor, member of the then Home Missions and Evangelism Department, and assistant to the manager of the Nazarene Publishing House. Just a few weeks before he died in 2000, he determined which books he would donate to BIM. Books in Mission has shipped Rev. Bowes's contribution of 4,426 books around the world to equip pastors for ministry. In a sense, the ministry of Rev. Bowes continues, not terminated by death.

Since its beginning in 1986, Books in Mission has mailed more than 269,000 pieces of literature to schools in 47 countries. These resources help train pastors who in turn equip the saints for works of service. The kingdom of God advances as the truth of God is planted and watered and cultivated through the written word—*words of life and love.*

6

WORDS OF
OUR FAITH

Where to begin? The apostle John sorted the memories, slowly organizing and setting the order. He picked up the stylus, only to lay it back on the table. So much to say.

John remembered the early days. What exhilaration! One moment he sat in a boat mending fishing nets; the next he walked beside Jesus as expanding crowds surged around them. Then there was the day John saw Jesus in dazzling white clothes and the voice from heaven announced Jesus as God's Son. Wow! But John knew he must do more than stimulate the imagination of the reader.

With some embarrassment, John remembered how he and his brother, James, were called the Sons of Thunder. He winced as he thought about threatening to call fire from heaven to destroy the city that rejected Jesus. He recalled the indignant looks when he and James asked for special privileges. John knew he deserved the rebuke that followed. But John felt uncomfortable making the book so autobiographical.

As John sat contemplating what he would write, he knew the most important thing he could do would be to testify "that Jesus is the Christ [Messiah], the Son of God" (John 20:31). John wanted people to believe. So he set out to record the miraculous signs that unmistakably identify Jesus as the Savior of the world.

John picked up the stylus and wrote about turning water to wine in Cana, healing the official's son in Capernaum, feeding the 5,000 near Bethsaida, walking on the Sea of Galilee, and cleansing 10 lepers in Samaria. John thought about the greatest sign of all, the one that caused him to believe. Jesus is alive! Jesus is the Christ!

John did more than prepare a narrative. He wrote about God. He explained that "the Word became flesh and made his dwelling among us" (John 1:14). In the same way, a theologian writes about God. "At the most elementary level, the linguistic meaning of *theology* is 'logos of theos,' words about God. Marianne Micks has refined this simple statement somewhat by defining theology as 'disciplined thinking about God.'"[1]

Theological Books

Beginning with H. Orton Wiley who wrote the three-volume set of books titled *Christian Theology*, published between 1940 and 1943, the Church of the Nazarene has been blessed with many writers who had the ability to clearly "provide rational formulation of our Christian beliefs."[2] Mildred Bangs Wynkoop, Richard Taylor, J. Kenneth Grider, William Greathouse, and others pondered the great mysteries of God, then wrote about what they only started to understand.

In the foreword to *Grace, Faith, and Holiness,*

the Board of General Superintendents of the Church of the Nazarene wrote, "It is imperative that these theological expressions be stated in the language and thought forms of every new generation if the life of the church is to be nurtured and sustained. While Christian truths remain constant, their mode of presentation varies and the means of comprehending them must be current in order to be relevant."[3]

One of the responsibilities of World Mission Literature Ministries is to assist in printing theological literature for all the languages represented in the work of the Church of the Nazarene around the world. Disciples will build a firm foundation of faith and congregations will soar to new spiritual heights as the timeless truth of God is presented in familiar "language and thought forms."

A Theological Textbook in Russian

Russians are passionate readers. People with a book are visible in many public places and book kiosks do a brisk business. Many countries that were part of the former Soviet Union have a literacy rate of 98-99 percent, higher than the literacy rates of the United States and Canada (95-96 percent).

During the time Communists governed, however, books were in short supply, especially religious books. In the first 70 years of Communism in Russia, 1917-1986, government leaders authorized only 450,000 copies of the Bible or New Testament for distribution. That is an average of about 6,400 Bibles per year in a country that spans 11 time zones. The situation changed quickly with the collapse of the iron curtain. In 1987-1988, religious groups distributed 1.3 million copies of the Bible. In 1989 the count soared to 6 million. The people who walked in darkness were eager for the light.

Not only did the Communists ban Christian books, they closed seminaries. Except for three schools to train Orthodox clergy, all formal pastoral training in the former Soviet Union ceased with the rise of Communism.

The Communist regime herded all Protestant denominations into one state-sponsored organization, the Union of Evangelical Baptists. Denominational distinctives faded with the forced amalgamation. To be identified as a Protestant had dire consequences, including the denial of an opportunity for higher education.

When the Church of the Nazarene began ministry in Russia in 1992, Nazarene missionaries found a dearth of Christian literature and scholars. Given the Russians' love of literature, the pioneer missionaries resolved early to provide Holiness literature for training pastors and theological educators in Christian doctrine.

Grace, Faith, and Holiness **was the first systematic theology book ever printed in the history of Russia.**

The Russian people, too, needed literature to help them understand the place of the Church of the Nazarene within Christianity. Since they were most familiar with the Russian Orthodox Church, that was often their reference point from which to evaluate the doctrine and practices of the Church of the Nazarene. Literature that clearly presented the beliefs of the Church of the Nazarene would begin to answer the questions the people had about the denomination.

In 1995 World Mission Literature Ministries received permission from Nazarene Publishing House to prepare a Russian edition of *Grace, Faith, and Holiness* by H. Ray Dunning. The English version of this book is more than 600 pages organized according to the three Persons of the Trinity: the doctrines of God the Sovereign, the doctrines of God the Savior, the doctrines of God the Spirit. Early in the book Dunning acknowledged that he approaches theology from a philosophical perspective, something that made his book a good fit for a person trained in the Russian educational system. *Grace, Faith, and Holiness* might not work as well in a culture with a different learning style, but it was perfect for the Russian context since the people thrive on the analytical process. The literature coordinator made the decision that this volume would be the first theological textbook translated into Russian by the Church of the Nazarene. They were to discover later that *Grace, Faith, and Holiness* was the first systematic theology book ever printed in the history of Russia.

But who could do such a monumental task? No missionary had the linguistic skill to even begin the process. There were no holiness theologians in the country who could help. Even other Protestants were not equipped to assist since they often had been denied higher education and access to contemporary Christian literature.

The Nazarene literature committee turned to

Bibles for Everyone, a Christian publishing company in St. Petersburg, Russia. Bibles for Everyone agreed to manage the massive task of producing the theological textbook for the Church of the Nazarene. The leaders of the publishing company asked that the Nazarenes pray fervently for them as they undertook this immense, complicated project.

The company contracted with professional translators to begin the work. Quickly they discovered that some theological terms did not have Russian equivalents. Seventy years of communist oppression resulted in a limited Russian theological vocabulary. They realized that to translate accurately the text, they needed to invent new Russian words. They were not only creating a new book, they were also building a lexicon.

Bibles for Everyone hired a philologist, a specialist in the history of a language, as a consultant. The Russian philologist helped the translators create theological terms that were consistent with the Russian language as it developed over the centuries. With a new lexicon in hand, the translators continued their work.

Nazarene missionary Nikolaj Sawatzky, the co-chair of the Commonwealth of Independent States (CIS) Literature Committee, guided the whole project. When the philologist made a suggestion, Nikolaj would evaluate it to be sure it captured the essence of Christian theology. He reviewed the work of the translators to confirm the final product reflected the nuances of Wesleyan theology. Finally, two years after beginning the project, the Russian edition of *Grace, Faith, and Holiness* came off the press on June

**Dr. Ray Hendrix with a copy of *Grace, Faith, and Holiness*
in the Russian language**

10, 1997, the first of several theological textbooks to
be printed in Russia.

About the time the Russian literature committee launched the *Grace, Faith, and Holiness* project,
Colorado Springs First Church of the Nazarene em-
barked on a major stewardship campaign. The congregation carried a large indebtedness that it wanted
to reduce. There were building maintenance issues
and ministry opportunities that needed attention.
Being a mission-minded congregation and wanting
to keep priorities in order, they looked for a special
world mission project they could incorporate in the
stewardship campaign. They were attracted to a lit-

erature project because a book is something tangible with a long shelf life. As a firstfruits offering, the initial $10,000 received in the stewardship program paid most of the expenses to translate and publish the Russian edition of *Grace, Faith, and Holiness*.

Other congregations and individuals have adopted projects through World Mission Literature Ministries. In memory of Gertrude Phillips, her family and friends sponsored the publication of *Life Can Have True Meaning* and *Basic Bible Studies for New and Growing Christians* in Macedonian. Mrs. Phillips' husband, Dr. E. S. Phillips, was the director of the Nazarene missions department from 1964 to 1973. The Portland, Oregon, Columbia Ridge Church of the Nazarene included the publication of the Arabic edition of a teen devotional book, *Spending Time with God*, as part of its Faith Promise budget one year. Sunday School classes and Vacation Bible Schools have adopted special projects. Districts and individuals have been champions of literature. These gifts permit World Mission Literature to publish more books of life and love.

After publication, the distribution of the Russian edition of *Grace, Faith, and Holiness* began. Every Nazarene pastor in Russia has a copy. Several seminaries adopted it as a textbook. Christian bookstores in Russia stock it.

Missions in the Church of the Nazarene has come full circle.

In 2002 the Nazarene missionaries in Russia received a letter from a man they did not know. He lived in a part of the country where the Church of the

Nazarene is yet to plant a church. After reading *Grace, Faith, and Holiness,* this man wanted to know more about the Church of the Nazarene. A theological textbook caused this man to seek more information on the organization and ministries of the denomination.

An International Church

H. T. Reza served as the first director of the Spanish Department, the predecessor to World Mission Literature Ministries. In his book, *Reza: His Life and Times,* Franklin Cook provided a perspective on the momentous impact of the creation of the Spanish Department. He wrote, "Some feel that the establishment of the Spanish Department in 1946 was the first real test of internationalization in the Church of the Nazarene. Before and during World War II, the Church of the Nazarene was primarily an American church with certain international interests. Even after World War II, for many years, very few had the concept of an international church or understood what it meant. Some of the practical demands made in the creation of a Spanish Department; some of the racial and cultural biases that were revealed; some of the crosscurrents of philosophical ideas that were generated assisted eventually in developing a concept of internationalization."[4]

Missions in the Church of the Nazarene has come full circle. For years the United States and Canada were sending countries. Now these two countries are receiving missionaries from other world areas. That is true with literature printed in

Russia. Books from Russia are coming to the United States for use in Russian-language congregations.

In the Commonwealth of Independent States, which includes Russia, the Church of the Nazarene has nine theological education extension centers with about 170 students enrolled. The missionaries are working to help persons for whom Russian is their native language to become the next generation of professors of biblical and theological studies. Several are in a master's degree program at Nazarene Theological Seminary, and some may go on for doctoral studies. In the next decade, the scholars for whom the Russian edition of *Grace, Faith, and Holiness* was their first theological text may be writing theological treatises of their own. When that day comes, English-speaking theologians will need the Russian books translated so as to benefit from their insights and words about God.

1. H. Ray Dunning, *Grace, Faith, and Holiness* (Kansas City: Beacon Hill Press of Kansas City, 1988), 23-24.

2. Dunning, 9.

3. Dunning, 6-7.

4. Franklin Cook, *Reza: His Life and Times* (Kansas City: Beacon Hill Press of Kansas City, 1988), 143.

AFTERWORD
GOD *IS* SPEAKING

God and words just seem to go together. The hymn "Thanks to God Whose Word Was Spoken"[1] (*Sing to the Lord*, No. 686) captures how God has been revealed to us. Stanza one reminds us that in Genesis 1 we repeatedly hear "and God said." God spoke the word and the universe was created. An echo of John 1:14, stanza two, reminds us that "The Word became flesh and made his dwelling among us." The Holy Scriptures are the theme of stanza three, the "living and active" Word of God (Heb. 4:12). Each stanza ends with the litany that God has spoken.

God *has* spoken. Our proclamation of the gospel echoes the message that God initiated in the revelation we received. We restate the Word of God in words understood by the very persons Jesus came to offer life that is abundant and eternal.

At the beginning of the 21st century we are in the midst of a technological revolution. In the years to come we will find new opportunities open to the church because of today's innovations.

Print-on-demand books will change the way publishers deliver books to their

> **With more literature in digital form in the future, we will probably speak more of the *written word* and less of the *printed page*.**

customers. Companies are developing production machines that may someday become as familiar to shoppers as the bank cash machine. A person interested in a book will be able to select a title at a kiosk. Once payment is made, the machine will access an electronic file where the book is stored, print the book's pages on a laser printer, print the cover in color, bind the book, and trim it to size. Like a vending machine, the print-on-demand book will slide down the delivery chute about 12 minutes later.

In the future more literature may be delivered on CD-ROM, thus reducing the need to print traditional books. The user simply puts the CD-ROM in a computer and reads the text on the screen. If the consumer wants a printed copy, he or she simply uses a printer connected to the computer. A few companies have been experimenting with small handheld computers designed specifically as electronic books. With more literature in digital form in the future, we will probably speak more of the *written word* and less of the *printed page*.

The Internet opens many exciting possibilities. E-mail speeds messages around the world in seconds. Workers in several countries can work on a single project through computer networks. A computer user in one country can access a computer file even though it is on a host computer thousands of miles away. Many more creative methods will emerge because of the Internet.

In addition to the new opportunities available because of technological advances, political changes will open doors for the church. Consider the Eastern Euro-

APPENDIX

Languages of Print Materials*
World Mission Regions, Church of the Nazarene
World Mission Literature Ministries
as of June 1, 2003

Key: AF, Africa; AP, Asia-Pacific; CA, Caribbean; EU, Eurasia; MC, Mexico/Central America; SA: South America

Language	Region	Language	Region	Language	Region
Afrikaans	AF	Haitian (Creole)	CA	Macedonian	EU
Albanian	EU	Herero	AF	Makua	AF
Amharic	AF	Hindi	EU	Malagasy	AF
Arabic	EU	Hungarian	EU	Malayan	AF
Aymara	SA	Ilocano	AP	Malaysian	AP
Bahasa Indonesian	AP	Ilonggo	AP	Manipuri	EU
Bangla	EU	Italian	EU	Marathi	EU
Bemba	AF	Japanese	AP	Mbukushu	AF
Bengali	EU	Kannada	EU	Mul	AF
Bulgarian	EU	K'ekchí	MC	Ndebele	AF
Burmese	AP	Khmer	AP	Oriya	EU
Cebuano	AP	Kinyarwanda	AF	Pedi	AF
Chichewa	AF	Korean	AP	Pokomchi	MC
Chokwe	AF	Kwangali	AF	Portuguese	AF, EU, SA
Danish	EU	Lahu	AP	Quechua	SA
Dutch	EU	Lam	AF	Quiché	SA
Efik	AF	Lamba	AF	Rabinal-Achi	MC
Fijian	AP	Lingala	AF	Romanian	EU
French	AF, CA, EU	Luganda	AF	Russian	EU
German	EU	Luo	AF	Samoan	AP
Greek	EU	Luvale	AF	Sena	AF
		Luyankole	AF	Setswana	AF

Shangaan	AF	Tamil	EU	Tumbuka	AF
Shona	AF	Telugu	EU	Twi	AF
Siswati	AF	Thado	EU	Urdu	EU
Sotho	AF	Thai	AP	Venda	AF
Spanish	CA, EU,	Tok Pisin	AP	Wahgi	AP
	MC, SA	Tonga	AP	Waray-Waray	AP
Swahili	AF	Tsonga	AF	Xhosa	AF
Tagalog	AP	Tswana	AF	Zulu	AF

---

*Languages in creative access areas are not listed for security reasons.